BRIGHT IDEA BOOKS

JORDAN Peele

by Samantha S. Bell

CAPSTONE PRESS
a capstone imprint

Bright Idea Books are published by Capstone Press
1710 Roe Crest Drive, North Mankato, Minnesota 56003
www.mycapstone.com

Library of Congress Cataloging-in-Publication Data
Library of Congress Cataloging-in-Publication Data is available on the Library of Congress website.
ISBN: 978-1-5435-5793-0 (library hardcover)
978-1-5435-6038-1 (paperback)
978-1-5435-5825-8 (eBook PDF)

Editorial Credits
Editor: Claire Vanden Branden
Designer: Becky Daum
Production Specialist: Colleen McLaren

Photo Credits
Alamy: Richard Ellis, 17; AP Images: Vince Bucci/Invision, cover; iStockphoto: TomasSereda, 11; Newscom: Byron Purvis/AdMedia, 18; Rex Features: Cindylou/Monkeypaw Prods./Martel & Roberts Prods./Kobal, 21, David Buchan/Variety, 8–9, David Fisher, 5, New Line Cinema/Principato-Young/Kobal, 24–25, Stephen Lovekin, 23; Shutterstock Images: CREATISTA, 30–31, Dfree, 26–27, Kathy Hutchins, 6–7, Kathy Hutchins, 14, lev radin, 12–13

Printed in the United States of America.
PA48

TABLE OF CONTENTS

CHAPTER 1

MAKING
History

Everyone in the crowd was standing and clapping. Jordan Peele just won an Academy Award.

Peele made a horror movie called *Get Out*. The movie won for Best Original Screenplay. Peele made history. He was the first African-American to win this award. Peele wrote and **directed** *Get Out*.

Peele with his Academy Award on March 4, 2018

Peele and the stars of *Get Out*, Daniel Kaluuya (left) and Allison Williams (right)

6

Peele never thought he would accomplish something like this. His hard work had paid off. He had started as an actor and comedian. Now he is an award-winning **screenwriter**.

Peele gave speeches after he won awards for *Get Out*.

A BIG HIT

Peele wanted to scare people. He wanted to make them think too. *Get Out* is about **racism**. The movie was a huge success. It made a lot of money. People loved it. The movie was also **nominated** for other awards.

THE ACADEMY AWARDS

The Academy Awards are the highest awards in film in the United States. Winners are given a gold statue. It is called an Oscar.

CHAPTER 2

GROWING
Up

Peele was born on February 21, 1979. He is **biracial**. His mother is white. His father was African-American. This made Peele feel like an outsider sometimes. He was not sure where he fit in. His father left when Peele was young. Peele grew up with just his mother.

Peele grew up in New York City, New York.

Peele joined TADA! Youth Theater in 1991. He now serves on its board of directors.

A NEW INTEREST

Peele started acting in fifth grade.

He really liked it.

HIGH SCHOOL MUSICALS

Peele was a member of the TADA! Youth Theater. The group performs **musicals** for students and families.

Peele says that scary stories became his strength after he scared his classmates around a fire.

Sometimes Peele watched scary movies. They frightened him a lot. One day, he went on a school trip. The students sat around a campfire. Peele told scary stories to the other students. He found out he liked telling stories.

Peele had a dream at 13 years old. He wanted to win an Academy Award someday.

CHAPTER 3

A STRONG
Start

Peele often practiced speaking like other people as a child. He became good at **impersonations**.

After high school, Peele attended college. He went to Sarah Lawrence College in New York. Peele wanted to work with puppets. Then he began doing **improv**. He also liked doing comedy.

Peele decided to leave college. He wanted a career in comedy. He joined an improv group. The group traveled to Chicago to perform. There Peele met Keegan-Michael Key. Key was a comedian too. They became good friends.

Peele started his comedy career at Second City in Chicago. This is a famous comedy club.

Key (left) and Peele enjoy making each other laugh.

A BIG BREAK

In 2003, Peele and Key both tried out for *MADtv*. This was a **sketch comedy** show that aired once a week. They were both hired.

Peele played many different people on the show. Some were celebrities. Some were musicians. He soon became a star on the show.

Peele often impersonated
President Barack Obama.

CHAPTER 4

COMEDY
Stars

MADtv ended five years later. The two

friends started their own show in 2012.

They called it *Key and Peele*. It aired on MTV.

The show covered things such as race
and **gender**. It made viewers laugh.
It also made them think about problems
in the world. The show won several awards.

Key and Peele won an Emmy
award in 2016 for *Key and Peele*.
The award was for Outstanding
Variety Sketch Series.

THE BIG SCREEN

Then Peele and Key wanted to make their own movie. That dream came true in 2016. They made an action comedy called *Keanu*. Peele's second film was *Get Out*. He realized he liked directing more than acting.

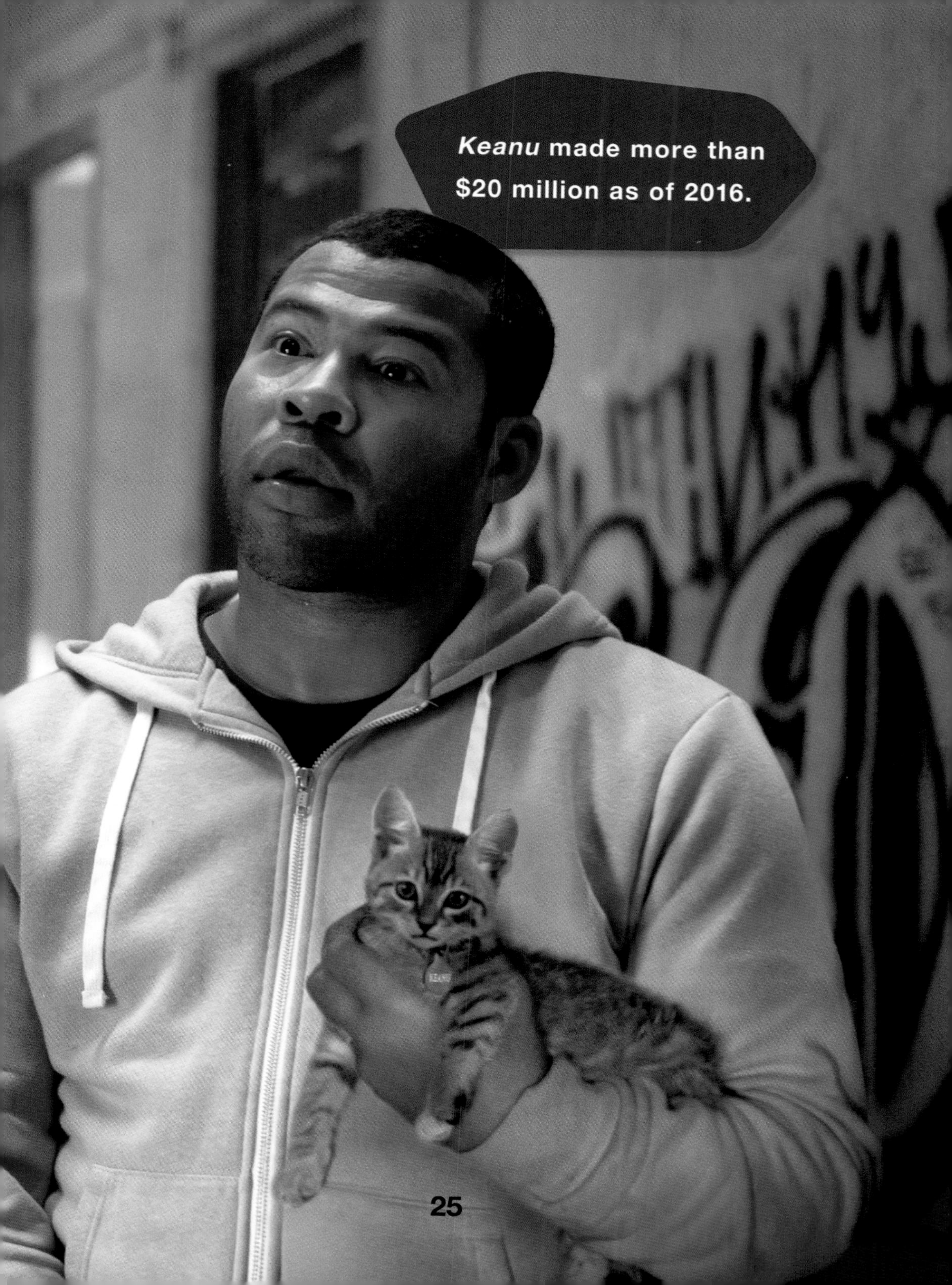

Keanu made more than $20 million as of 2016.

Peele married Chelsea Peretti in 2016. They have one child together, a son named Beaumont.

Now Peele has a new dream. He wants to make more scary movies. His movies will be frightening and funny. They will also cover real problems in the world.

MONKEYPAW PRODUCTIONS

Peele created his own **production company**. Its shows and movies will combine real-world problems with humor. It is called Monkeypaw Productions.

GLOSSARY

biracial
having parents of two
different races

direct
to be in charge of actors and
crew members for a movie,
play, or musical

gender
the behaviors or traits usually
associated with either males
or females

impersonation
pretending to be
another person

improv
a form of theater, often
comedy, in which most or
all of the performance is
unplanned

musical
a play that tells a story
with songs

nominated
to have been chosen as a
candidate for something

production company
a company that provides
money for TV shows or
movies to be made

racism
the belief that certain races
are superior to others

screenwriter
a person who writes scripts
for movies, including
instructions on how a movie
should be acted and filmed

sketch comedy
a show that is made up
of short funny stories

TIMELINE

1979: Jordan Peele is born.

2003: Peele meets Keegan-Michael Key.

2012: Peele and Key star in *Key and Peele* on MTV.

2016: Peele marries comedian Chelsea Peretti.

2017: Peele and Peretti have a baby boy named Beaumont Gino Peele.

2018: Peele's movie *Get Out* wins an Academy Award for Best Original Screenplay.

ACTIVITY

TRY IMPROV

Improv is a type of acting that does not use a script. Instead, the actors make up the scene as they go along. The scenes are usually funny.

YOUTH
theater

You can try improv with your friends or family. First, choose two or more people to act out the scene. Everyone else will be the audience.

Next, have a person in the audience suggest a location, an action, an object, or a career. The actors must then use that suggestion to create the scene.

If you need any inspiration, check out other groups online. Improv4Kids puts videos of improv shows and comedy on YouTube. Ask an adult to help you find one of these videos on the company's YouTube channel.

FURTHER RESOURCES

Interested in acting? Try some of these scenes and plays:

Harbison, Lawrence. *The Best Scenes for Kids Ages 7–15*. Milwaukee, WI: Applause Theare & Cinema Books, 2015.

PBS Zoom Playhouse: Act Up and Put On a Play
https://pbskids.org/zoom/activities/playhouse

Wonder what improv looks and sounds like? Visit this website to see some kids in action:

http://www.thecomedykids.com

Want to practice improvising? Try this activity:

Bay Area Discovery Museum: Dubbing
https://creativitycatapult.org/activity/dubbing

INDEX

7

YOUR LAND
AND
MY LAND
The Middle East

We Visit

ISRAEL

Laya

Saul

Mitchell Lane
PUBLISHERS
P.O. Box 196
Hockessin, Delaware 19707

CYPRUS

Beirut
LEBANON

Haifa
ISRAEL

Port
Said

Jerusalem

SYRIA

Dead Sea

YOUR LAND
AND
MY LAND
The Middle
East

Afghanistan
Iran
Iraq
Israel
Kuwait
Oman
Pakistan
Saudi Arabia
Turkey
Yemen

TREA Massawa
ra ★

Mitchell Lane
PUBLISHERS

Printing   1   2   3   4   5   6   7   8   9

Library of Congress Cataloging-in-Publication Data
Saul, Laya.
 We visit Israel / by Laya Saul.
     p. cm. — (Your land and my land: the Middle East)
 Includes bibliographical references and index.
 ISBN 978-1-58415-957-5 (library bound)
 1. Israel—Juvenile literature. I. Title.
 DS126.5.S227 2012
 956.94—dc23
                                                                        2011024706

eBook ISBN: 9781612280981

PUBLISHER'S NOTE: This story is based on the author's years of living in Israel and on her extensive research, which she believes to be accurate. Documentation of this research is on page 60.

The Internet sites referenced herein were active as of the publication date. Due to the fleeting nature of some web sites, we cannot guarantee they will all be active when you are reading this book.

To reflect current usage, we have chosen to use the secular era designations BCE ("before the common era") and CE ("of the common era") instead of the traditional designations BC ("before Christ") and AD (*anno Domini,* "in the year of the Lord").

PLB

Contents

Introduction

In the vast region that is known as the Middle East, there is a small country called Israel. It shares borders with Lebanon, Syria, Jordan, and Egypt. Its western edge is a coastline on the deep blue Mediterranean Sea. At the southernmost tip is the Red Sea (which isn't red at all).

This tiny country has such a rich history that it continually draws the attention of the world. For thousands of years, nations have battled for control over the land that is now known as Israel. The Turks, Babylonians, Romans, and more came and conquered it, and then faded away into ancient history. After the Muslims captured the city of Jerusalem in 1076, knights of the Crusades came to take it back for Christianity. Throughout the turnovers and bloody wars, the Jews remained, and their love and connection to the land has continued to hold strong.

What is it about this small country that makes it so special? What is it about the history of this place—a desert filled with snakes and scorpions, with a sea so full of salt that nothing can live in it—that has made so many empires want to own it? Just what makes so many people from around the world want to visit and touch this land? Let's find out as we explore the history, culture, people, and sights of the land of Israel.

Hebron, one of the four holy cities of Israel, is home to the Cave of the Patriarchs (the large rectangular stone building in the center of the photograph). Hebron is connected to the element of earth. The other holy cities are Tiberias, on the Sea of Galilee (water); Safed, known as the place of the mystics (air); and Jerusalem, the city of gold (fire).

The Land of Milk and Honey—Ancient and Spiritual

"Throw him into the furnace!" bellowed the ruler Nimrod. Then, according to a Jewish text called the Talmud, a boy was thrown into the fire. Miraculously, the child survived. What did he do? He defied the belief of the times and even his own father by denying that statues, idols, and rulers were gods. He declared idolatry a lie, and proclaimed that there is one omnipotent God who rules the world. That child grew up to become the man many people know as Abraham.

The history of the modern state of Israel begins in ancient times, in the Hebrew Bible (known by Christians as the Old Testament), with the story of Abraham. He said that there is only one, true God: not a god that is an old man who sits on a throne somewhere in the clouds, as the ancient Greeks and Romans believed, but rather "All that is, all that will be, and all that ever was," beyond human intelligence and understanding, even beyond imagination. In the Bible, Abraham talks with God, and God sends Abraham on a journey to a new land. They make a covenant (a binding agreement) that would last for all time. The Bible also records the purchase of the land where Abraham would bury his wife, Sarah, in what is now the city of Hebron. He was later buried there, too, as were his son and grandson and their wives. That was around 4,000 years ago. That place, called the Cave of the Patriarchs, still exists and is still visited by tens of thousands of people each year. The descendants of Abraham—the Children of Israel—also still exist. They are the Jewish people.

Moses with the Ten Commandments by Rembrandt, 1659

The story in the Bible continues with the small nation of Jews going to Egypt to escape a famine. They eventually become slaves. With miracles from above, and led by Moses, the Israelites are delivered from slavery in Egypt and into the Sinai Desert. As the Israelites are gathered at the base of Mount Sinai, Moses receives two tablets (according to oral tradition, they are made of sapphire) inscribed with the Ten Commandments—God's rules for life. Then, with a pillar of cloud by day and a pillar of fire by night, God leads them to the Land of Israel. Since that time, the Jewish people have remained physically and spiritually connected to the land.

After the Jews re-entered ancient Israel, King Solomon built the Holy Temple in Jerusalem. This is where the ark of the covenant, which held the original tablets that Moses brought down from Mount Sinai, was housed, and where Jews came to pray. The Temple was destroyed once by the Assyrian Greeks, and after seventy years was rebuilt. Later, the conquering Romans destroyed the second Temple. Most of the Jews were exiled, and they spread throughout the world. In biblical times, the Philistines were the enemies of the Jews. As an insult, after the Land of Israel was conquered, the name of the land was changed to Palestina, meaning "land of the Philistines."

The areas of Jewish settlement outside the land of Israel are called the Diaspora, from the Greek word for "dispersed" or "scattered." Jewish communities developed, held together by the biblical laws that the people observed. No matter where they were in the world, they studied the Torah, observed the same holidays, and prayed the same prayers. For more than two thousand years, no matter where they were, they continued to face Jerusalem during their daily prayers.

Despite their positive outlook, their troubles did not end. It seemed that wherever they began to flourish, anti-Semitism—hatred of the Jews—followed. Jews were often the target of forced religious conversion and other kinds of persecution. Sometimes they were expelled, as happened during the Spanish Inquisition. During this time of terror, the Catholic rulers of Spain interrogated and tortured Jews and others who had been forced to convert to Catholicism. They wanted to make sure that those who had converted were not secretly observing their traditional customs. Many were killed, and ultimately the Jews were expelled from the country altogether in 1492.

The Holy Land

Israel is holy not only to the Jews. For Christians, it has special meaning as the land of Jesus—who they believe is the direct son of God and who was the founder of Christianity. Christian pilgrims travel to modern Israel to enjoy the many sites written about in the Christian Bible (the Old and New Testaments), such as Bethlehem, where Jesus was born; Nazareth, where he grew up and worked as a carpenter; the Sea of Galilee, where he fished and is said to have walked on water; and Golgotha, where he was crucified and laid in a tomb.

The Muslims consider Jerusalem a holy city as well. The same site that is holy for the Jews, the Temple Mount (the site of the Holy Temple), is also the place where the Muslims built the Dome of the Rock. It is said that the Muslim prophet Muhammad ascended to Heaven from that spot. There is a controversy about whether to call the Dome of the Rock a shrine (a place that houses a sacred object) or a mosque (a Muslim place of worship). Either way, Muslims consider it holy.

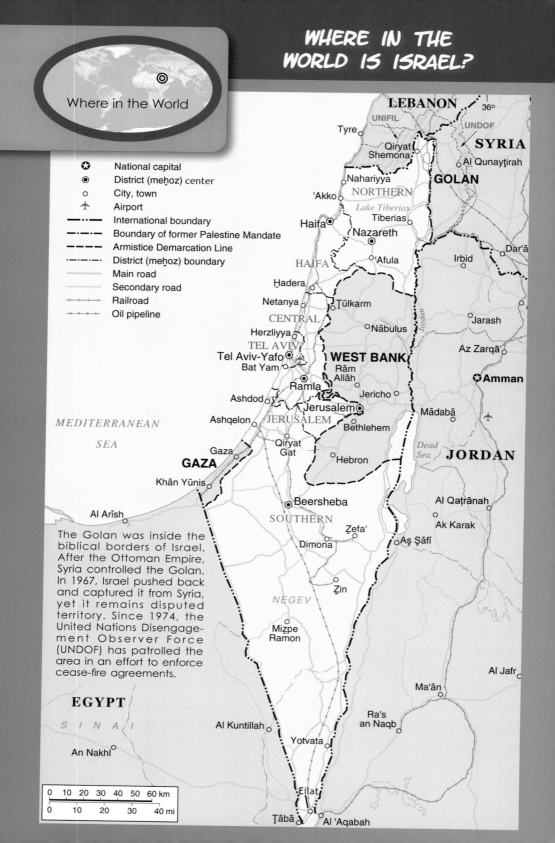

Where in the World

- ✪ National capital
- ◉ District (meḥoz) center
- ○ City, town
- ✈ Airport
- ▬·▬·▬ International boundary
- ▬··▬··▬ Boundary of former Palestine Mandate
- ▬ ▬ ▬ Armistice Demarcation Line
- ▬····▬····▬ District (meḥoz) boundary
- ━━━ Main road
- ─── Secondary road
- ┼┼┼┼ Railroad
- ◆◆◆◆ Oil pipeline

LEBANON   36°
UNIFIL   UNDOF
Tyre   Qiryat   SYRIA
            Shemona
                        Al Qunayṭirah
        Nahariyya   GOLAN
'Akko   NORTHERN
Haifa   Lake Tiberias
        Tiberias
        Nazareth   Dar'ā
HAIFA   Afula   Irbid
Ḥadera
Netanya   Ṭūlkarm   Jarash
CENTRAL   Nābulus
Herzliyya   Az Zarqā'
TEL AVIV
Tel Aviv-Yafo   WEST BANK
Bat Yam   Rām   ✪ Amman
        Allāh
Ramla   Jericho
Ashdod   Jerusalem   Mādabā
Ashqelon JERUSALEM Dead JORDAN
        Bethlehem   Sea
MEDITERRANEAN Qiryat
        Gat   Hebron
SEA   Gaza
GAZA
Khān Yūnis   Al Qaṭrānah
                    Ak Karak
Al Arīsh   Beersheba
        SOUTHERN   Zefa'
        Dimona   Aṣ Ṣāfī

Zin

NEGEV   Al Jafr

The Golan was inside the
biblical borders of Israel.
After the Ottoman Empire,
Syria controlled the Golan.
In 1967, Israel pushed back
and captured it from Syria,
yet it remains disputed
territory. Since 1974, the
United Nations Disengage-
ment Observer Force
(UNDOF) has patrolled the
area in an effort to enforce
cease-fire agreements.

Mizpe
Ramon   Ma'ān

EGYPT
SINAI   Ra's
            an Naqb
Al Kuntillah
        Yotvata
An Nakhl

0 10 20 30 40 50 60 km
0   10   20   30   40 mi

Eilat
Ṭābā Al 'Aqabah

ISRAEL FACTS AT A GLANCE

Full name: State of Israel, also called Israel

Official language: Hebrew; Arabic is also officially used for the Arab minority. English is widely known

Population: Approximately 7,473,052 (July 2010 est.)

Land area: 8,019 square miles (20,770 square kilometers); roughly the size of New Jersey

Capital: Jerusalem

Government: Parliamentary Democracy

Ethnic makeup: Jews (76.4 percent), non-Jews (mostly Muslim: 23.6 percent)

Exports: Machinery and equipment, software, cut diamonds, agricultural products, chemicals, textiles and apparel

Imports: Raw materials, military equipment, investment goods, rough diamonds, fuels, grain, consumer goods

Agricultural products: Citrus fruits, vegetables, cotton; beef, poultry, dairy products

Average temperatures: Vary depending on the region: in August, Jerusalem can be as cool as 66°F (19°C), while in Eilat it can get as hot as 104°F (40°C); January ranges from 43°F to 70°F (6 to 21°C)

Average rainfall: Varies depending on the region: from 3.9 to 44.4 inches (100 to 1,128 millimeters)

Highest point: Mount Hermon—9,232 feet (2,814 meters)

Lowest point: The Dead Sea (approximately –1,310 feet/ –400 meters)

Longest river: The Jordan River (157 miles/252 kilometers)

Flag: The Israeli flag has two blue stripes, one at the top and one at the bottom, with a blue Star of David in the middle, all on a white field. The stripes call to mind the prayer shawl, or tallith. The Hebrew words for "Star of David" are *Magen David,* which means "shield of David." David, from the Torah (the Hebrew Bible), was one of the greatest kings of ancient Israel. He referred to God as his shield, meaning that God protected him in battle. The six points of the star represent God's rule over the world from all directions (north, south, east, west, up, down).

National flower: Persian cyclamen (*Cyclamen persicum*)

National bird: Hoopoe (*Upupa epops*)

National tree: Olive (*Olea europaea*)

Sources: CIA—*The World Factbook:* "Israel." https://www.cia.gov/library/publications/the-world-factbook/geos/is.html; Aish.com, "Star of David" http://www.aish.com/jl/sp/k/48942436.html; Israel Tourism Guide: "Mount Hermon" http://tourism.index.co.il/siteFiles/1/60/260968.asp

Jewish immigrants arrive in Haifa aboard a refugee ship in 1948. They are waving the future flag of the state of Israel.

The Shaping of Modern Israel

While there has always been some Jewish presence in the region, the Jews began to return in greater numbers during what is now called the First Aliyah, from 1882 to 1903. This is when Jews from Eastern Europe and Russia who wanted to escape horrific pogroms (massacres of defenseless people) settled in the land. The Second Aliyah followed from 1904 to 1914, after more pogroms in Russia. *Aliyah* is a Hebrew word that means "ascending," or "going up"; this is how moving to the land of Israel is described by Jews, since it is such a holy place for them. *Aliyah* is the word still used when a Jew returns from the Diaspora to live in Israel.

During the First and Second Aliyahs, the land of Israel was under Turkish rule, controlled by the Ottoman Empire. World War I brought the Ottoman Empire to an end, and in 1917, the British Mandate over the land then called Palestine began. Under British rule, the country of Jordan was formed from British Mandate Palestine; and during this time, from 1919 to 1923, the Third Aliyah came from Poland, Russia, and Romania. The fourth wave arrived from 1924 to 1931.

Rising from the Ashes
In the late 1930s, Adolf Hitler and his Nazi Party rose to power in Germany with a vision to take over the world. His vision included what he called "the Final Solution," which meant rounding up and murdering all the Jews of Europe—men, women, children, and even babies. During World War II, he carried out one of history's worst

atrocities—the Holocaust. As the war was raging, Jews from all over Europe were herded to fields and concentration camps to be shot, gassed and burned, starved, or worked to death. The Nazis murdered approximately six million Jews during World War II.

After World War II and Hitler's defeat, the surviving Jews of Europe, devastated by their losses, faced new challenges. When some of them tried to return to their homes in Poland, Romania, and other countries, their neighbors made it clear that they were not welcome. The surviving Jews of Europe needed to find a home. There were quotas on how many Jews could immigrate to the United States, Canada, and other countries around the world. Many Jews wanted to return to Israel, the land of their ancestors, which was still under British rule when the war ended.

As the world began to heal after the war, the newly formed United Nations decided to divide the land that was called Palestine into two states, an Arab state and a Jewish state. The Jews would have an autonomous government. They agreed to the division of land, but the Arabs did not. From the moment the United Nations gave the Jews political sovereignty in 1948, five of its Arab neighbors attacked. With no organized army and hardly any weapons,

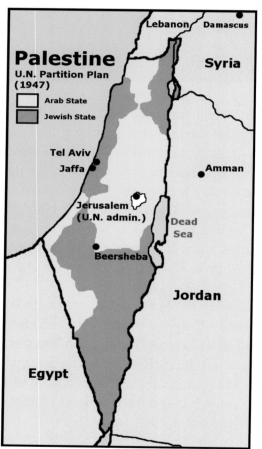

In 1947, the United Nations created a partition plan for two states, one Jewish and one Arab. The Jews living there accepted the plan, but the Arabs in Palestine and the surrounding countries rejected it.

the pioneers—Jews who had come to farm and build—and the survivors of the Holocaust now had to fight for their independence. Against all odds, Israel won. After two thousand years, the region began to flourish under Jewish rule once again.

In the more than sixty years since Israel gained independence in 1948, the country has been attacked by surrounding nations. Those who fought in the wars saw firsthand the miracles and wonder that helped the small nation prevail over its enemies. In 1956 the Sinai

On May 14, 1948, David Ben-Gurion gave a speech declaring the creation of the State of Israel. Hanging behind the panel of the People's Council and Zionist Executive is a photo of Theodor Herzl, who was a key builder and founder of the modern Zionist movement to build a Jewish State. Herzl famously declared, "If you will, it is no fairytale."

Campaign fought to stop terrorism. In 1967 the Six Day War was waged, with Syria attacking in the north and Egypt sending 100,000 troops in the south. The borders of the country changed during this war as Israel conquered the Golan Heights, the Sinai Peninsula, and other parcels of land. (The Sinai Peninsula was later returned to Egypt in exchange for Egypt's promise not to attack Israel.) Jerusalem, which had been divided until then, was united. Jews again had access to the Western Wall, the remaining outer wall from the ancient Holy Temple. In 1973, on Yom Kippur, the holiest day of the year for Jews, Syria and Egypt launched an attack that took Isarel by surprise.

There continue to be wars, negotiations, terrorist attacks, compromises, and challenges for the young nation. Several organizations and Arab countries have said they will settle for nothing less than the complete destruction of the Jewish state. Other countries, including the United States, have attempted to broker compromises that could bring peace to the Middle East, but the region remains in turmoil. Meanwhile, the people of Israel do their best to live and prosper, building communities and contributing to the world through innovations in medicine and technology.

Constant Controversy

People and governments have continued to argue over Israel's right to exist. Land that Israel won in wars—including Judea and Samaria (also called the West Bank) and the Golan Heights, as well as parts of Jerusalem—is under constant dispute. Israel even returned land that was won in war, such as the Sinai Desert and Gaza, hoping that they could trade land for peace. Still, despite the Jews' four-thousand-year history in the land, there are many who believe that the State of Israel should be abolished.

Within the country itself, there are many disagreements about how the country should be run: should it be a religious government or a secular government, politically conservative or liberal? One reason Israel stands out from its neighbors is that it is a democracy. Everyone can have a voice; everyone can be represented in government. Minorities and women serve in government. Even minorities who speak out against the very existence of the government to which they were elected

FYI FACT:

Jews whose ancestors lived in Eastern European countries during the Diaspora are called Ashkenazi (ahsh-keh-NAH-zee) Jews. Those whose ancestors lived in Spanish or Arabic countries are called Sephardic (seh-FAR-dik) Jews. The Jews from Ethiopia are called Beta Israel (meaning "house of Israel").

have the freedom to say what they want. However, elections are different in Israel than in other democracies, such as the United States, in that the people vote for the political party they want to run the country, not for individual politicians.

The Government

The government is a multiparty parliamentary democracy. It has three branches:

The Legislative Authority. The Parliament, called the Knesset (kuh-NEH-set), has 120 members who ___ ___tionally elected and serve for four years. Their main job is to ___ ___ ___laws). They also vote for the president, who serves f___ ___ ___ ___whose duties are mostly ceremonial.

The Executive Authority. T___ ___ ___ ___ ___rime minister, who serves a term ___ government (cabinet of m___ state. These ministers d___ members of the Knesse___

The Judicial System ___ be a system to make ___ by the president afte___ up of supreme co___ They are appoint___ justice system i___ status (such as___ tion of the r___ to the relig___ (Jewish) ___ recogniz___

The highest
Mount Hermon and no___
In summertime, there are hiki___
A strategic military post on Mo___
known for its state-of-the-art defense t___

thernmost point in Israel,
ski resort in the country.
ng trails to explore.
unt Hermon is
chnology.

A Mini Tour of Northern Israel

From modern architecture to ancient sites, there is plenty to see and experience in Israel. The natural beauty of hand-planted forests, the fertile coastal plain sown with crops, the stark desert vista, and the breezy beaches along the Mediterranean Sea await travelers and residents alike.

Winters in the north and on the coast are cool and rainy, but from springtime into early fall, there is no rainfall in Israel. That makes for a lot of summertime fun.

From the northernmost tip of Israel to the southernmost point, there is a variety of sights and activities. Whether you like nature or technology, strolling through museums, lounging on the beach, or playing sports, there is a lot to see and do.

MOUNT HERMON AND THE GOLAN: The highest elevation in Israel, Mount Hermon is located in the area of Golan on the border between Lebanon, Jordan, and Syria. The peaks of Mount Hermon have snow all year long. It has the most developed ski resort in the Middle East, with ski runs for all levels of skiers. Mount Hermon is usually covered in snow from December to April. Rarely is there snowfall in the rest of the country.

Mount Hermon has been part of Israel for over 40 years. The Golan Heights was captured by the Israel Defense Forces during the 1967 war. It is not a place where Syrians lived; it was used only for a place from which to attack Israel. There are still minefields there, and travelers must be careful to keep out of the marked areas to stay safe. Tourists can visit Syrian bunkers to help understand the history of the area. The Israeli farmlands below have rows of tall cypress trees at their edges that were planted in order to protect the farmers from gunfire by Syrian troops. A trip to the Golan today shows that Israel has planted trees all the way to the Syrian border.

Jeep tours are a fun and popular way to view the land up close. In the Golan, drivers must be careful, since wild boars and jackals often dart into the road.

To the west of the Golan is Hula Valley.

HULA VALLEY: Walking, biking, and exploring are all popular in this protected nature reserve. Birds such as pelicans, cranes, and ducks stop here during their flights north for the summer and south for the winter. A visit to a nature reserve introduces city kids to such wildlife as deer and ibex. Native to Israel is the hyrax, a small furry animal that is actually related to the elephant. Hyraxes live in both northern and southern Israel. The mongoose, another small mammal, is lively but shy and hunts snakes.

Heading a little way south is the small town of Safed.

Cranes in the Hula Valley. Twice a year, millions of birds stop in the Hula Valley wetlands and nature reserve on their migration routes. Thousands of birdwatchers, naturalists, and photographers come to watch and help preserve this international treasure.

SAFED: At the top of a mountain sits the peaceful city of Safed, the capital of Jewish mysticism—teachings from thousands of years ago of the deep and sometimes secret spiritual meanings of the Torah. The narrow cobblestone streets of the old city twist and turn past many art galleries, where tourists can see ceramics, jewelry, paintings, and sculptures. One kind of art there is microcalligraphy. The artists take a section of the Bible and in tiny letters copy the text, in Hebrew, into the shape of a picture that describes the story. Safed is famous for its cheese and candle factories, and for its variety of old synagogues, each with its stories of miracles. Just outside town are many hiking trails. At Bat Ya'ar Ranch are horseback riding adventures and a ropes course. Since Safed is on a mountain, there are great views all around. From one side Mount Hermon can be seen, and from the other, the Sea of Galilee and Tiberias.

TIBERIAS: Tiberias is situated on the shore of the Sea of Galilee, which is also called Lake Tiberias or the Kinneret (pronounced kee-NAYR-it). People enjoy boating, fishing, swimming, and windsurfing on the Sea of Galilee. There are even ships that set out for a night of dancing under the stars. A walk near the water will take visitors past rows of shops. Restaurants with views of the water and surrounding mountains offer delicious food, from fish to Chinese cuisine. The Sea of Galilee is where Jesus is said to have walked on water, so it is a favorite stop for Christian tourists. Nearby is the Mount of Beatitudes, where the famous Sermon on the Mount took place. Visitors can raft or kayak down the Jordan River to cool off during summer months.

Heading west on the way to the coast is Nazareth.

The Church of the Apostles, a Greek Orthodox church on the Sea of Galilee near Capernaum, is where Jesus chose his apostles.

NAZARETH: Another popular Christian tourist site is Nazareth, which has many churches and is said to be the place where Jesus spent his childhood. There is even an ancient Turkish bathhouse that is open to the public. Nazareth is the largest Arab city in Israel, with both Christian and Muslim Arabs.

Continuing west to the coast is Haifa.

Forests are not natural to Israel because the land is rocky or sandy. Since the days of the pioneers, starting in 1901, over 240 million trees have been planted in Israel by the Jewish National Fund to make the land breathe with green. Every year on the holiday of Tu B'Shvat—The New Year for the trees—people plant trees as part of the celebration.

HAIFA: Haifa is one of Israel's leading port cities, so this is a place to see giant ships coming in and going out to sea. Because it is on a mountain, the streets can be winding and steep. Carmel, a suburb of Haifa, has a feeling similar to the streets of San Francisco, California. One of the most-visited sites in Haifa is the Baha'i Temple (below), known for its gardens and views of the city.

The Technion, or Israel Institute of Technology, was founded in Haifa in 1912. Israel is known for advanced technology, and the Technion is a large part of that, issuing more than 12,000 college degrees in 2010!

Just outside of Haifa are the ruins of the Crusader castle at Atlit.

Let's travel south along the coast next to the blue-green water of the Mediterranean Sea.

At the center of Israel is the fast-paced city of Tel Aviv. Known for its beautiful Mediterranean beaches, it is also a place for great shopping, dining, universities, and high-tech industries. Like the rest of Israel, it is a diverse city, with mosques and churches as well as synagogues.

Chapter 4

A Mini Tour of Central and Southern Israel

The area along the coast—the coastal plain—is where the majority of the population in Israel lives. There is much to do and see. Tel Aviv is one of the most well known cities of Israel.

TEL AVIV-JAFFA: Tel Aviv has all the benefits of most big cities: a business center with high-rise buildings, a shopping haven, and a place where cafés and restaurants abound. It is the cultural center of Israel, with theater, dance, the Israel Philharmonic Orchestra, and more than twenty museums. This metropolis began modestly when six Jewish families started a neighborhood in Jaffa in 1906. The settlement was renamed Tel Aviv in 1909 and grew from there. Bordering the city are eight and a half miles (14 kilometers) of Mediterranean beaches.

Just outside of Tel Aviv in Holon is Israel Children's Museum. A popular exhibit called "Dialogue in the Dark" lets sighted people experience what it's like to be blind.

JERUSALEM: The city, both modern and ancient, is often called Jerusalem of Gold. Buildings of stone reflect golden sunsets, when the city takes on a special air and seems to glow. Nations have fought over Jerusalem for centuries. In the news, Jerusalem is often discussed. It is a city full of possibilities. Learn more about Jerusalem in chapter 8.

BETHLEHEM: Just south of Jerusalem is the biblical city of Bethlehem, important to Christians as the birthplace of Jesus. A silver star in the Church of the Nativity was placed over the manger where Jesus was laid (above). Bethlehem is also the location of a holy site for Jews: the Tomb of Rachel, wife of the biblical patriarch Jacob.

MODI'IN: Located near the modern city of Modi'in, where the Maccabees fought the historic battles that we know as the story of Chanukah, is Neot Kedumim—the Biblical Landscape Reserve in Israel. This unique nature reserve features hundreds of species of plants and animals mentioned in the Bible, such as acacia and willow. Other exhibits show wine presses, baths, and other tools and buildings used in biblical times. Nearby, in the city of Latrun, is Mini Israel, a park that contains a scale model of the entire country, featuring holy sites and many other points of interest.

REHOVOT: In the modern city of Rehovot, kids can explore the outdoor Clore Garden of Science at the Weizmann Institute of Science, where interactive, hands-on exhibits and activities demonstrate the principles of physics.

HEBRON: In the midst of the biblical Plains of Mamre lies Hebron, another of Israel's holiest cities. People come from far and wide to visit the Cave of the Patriarchs, burial place of the biblical Abraham and Sarah, Isaac and Rebecca, and Jacob and Leah. Tradition holds that Adam and Eve are also buried in Hebron.

DEAD SEA: The lowest place on earth, the Dead Sea is a favorite retreat for tourists and Israelis alike. The size of a small lake, the water is so full of salt that it does not support plant life or fish. Swimmers float without trying. There are also mud baths nearby, with special black clay that can be washed off with a swim. Spa products made from Dead Sea minerals are sold around the world.

Ein Gedi, near the Dead Sea, is among the protected nature reserves in Israel.

MITZPE RAMON: The unique, canyon-sized Ramon Crater (above), located in the Negev Desert in southern Israel, is a breathtaking sight. It was not formed from the impact of a meteorite; it is a natural desert formation. Tourists can take a jeep tour or a camel ride—from sitting for a photo to taking a camel safari into the desert. In this region, which is at the center of two nature reserves, visitors can see alpaca farms (below), enjoy thermal baths, practice archery, bike, or hike.

EILAT: Through the Negev Desert is the southernmost city on the Red Sea coast, Eilat. It stays warm even in the winter. Snorkeling, diving, kayaking, paddleboating, water skiing, and swimming with dolphins are just some of the things to do in Eilat. Eilat is on the migration route of birds that pass through the Sahara and Siberia.

Those who like to rough it can enjoy backpacking and camping; others might just go sunning on the beach. Whatever your preference, there is a lot to explore in Israel.

Kings City is a biblical theme park in Eilat that resembles a king's palace. The park is divided into four sections in what park management says will "convey to visitors an experience of a voyage in time through caves quarried in the rock, sailing through King Solomon's halls, and an abundance of interactive experiences."

While modern grocery stores and malls abound, people can also shop in open-air markets called *shuks*. They can find produce, housewares, clothing, candy, and spices.

Meet the People of Israel

Of the approximately 7.4 million people who live in Israel, over 75 percent are Jews and about 17 percent are Muslim. The Jewish majority is made up of a mix of Jews who have returned to the land from all around the world: the United States, Canada, Argentina, Colombia, Brazil, South Africa, Morocco, Tunisia, Yemen, Ethiopia, Europe, Russia, Australia, and India. Within the Arab population, the majority of Arabs are Muslim, but there are many Christian Arabs as well. There are also Bedouin and Druze.

Some of the people who live in Israel are religious and others are secular, meaning they do not observe religious practices. Whether religious or secular, Jewish, Muslim, Christian, Baha'i, or of any of the other religions that are represented, all people are free to practice (or not practice) their religion in Israel.

The official language of Israel is Hebrew. Arabic is also used for the Arab minority. English is very common around the country as well.

What Do They Eat in Israel?

One of the well-known exports of Israel is the produce—the abundant fruits of the land. Tourists regard them as among the tastiest in the world. Perhaps that is because Israel is so small that it can let fruits and vegetables ripen on the vine, since it takes only a few hours to truck them from any place in the country to another.

Nearly every grocery store has a selection of typical Middle Eastern salads or dips in the refrigerated section: hummus (creamy dip made from garbanzo beans), tahini (creamy dip made from sesame seeds), *matbuha* (a little spicy and like salsa: chunky tomato, pepper, and onion), and a variety of eggplant salads, such as *baba ganoush.* An array of these salads and some pita bread can make a whole meal, but the salads are usually just the beginning. One of the main "fast foods" of Israel is called falafel. These are like spicy meatballs, but they are not made with meat at all. They are made from ground-up garbanzo beans, which are fried and then stuffed into a pita pocket along with salads or dips. The other popular fast food is called *shwarma.* Instead of falafel, this pita bread sandwich is stuffed with spiced meat. If you like your food even spicier, you can add hot peppers or *schug* (pronounced *s-hoog*), but watch out, because these are hot!

The Israeli salad is simple but very tasty: tomatoes and cucumbers and sometimes red peppers, chopped small and mixed with salt, lemon juice, and olive oil.

Of course you'll find standard Western fare as well: hamburgers and fries or pizza. Besides fast food, there are many restaurants all across Israel serving almost any kind of food you can imagine. Israel has immigrants from all over the world, and many have brought their exotic foods and recipes, from sushi to spaghetti to barbecue.

Sufganiyah

It's not just the restaurants that are influenced by the many cultures that come together in Israel. Many of the home-cooked foods are influenced by the countries in which the people's grandparents lived. The Jews from Eastern Europe eat things like gefilte fish—a kind

34

of fish patty made with onions and other spices. The Jews who moved to Israel from some of the Arab countries prepare things like *malawa* or *jahnoon,* which are main-dish pastries. Nearly every bakery in Israel carries a variety of pastries called *bourekas.* These are not sweet, but are filled with potatoes or cheese. You can also find a nice rye bread that comes from the Russian traditional breads.

National Treasures

Children are precious treasures in Israel. Public schools educate Israeli children. Private schools can also receive money from the government to help with the costs. In high school, youths participate in testing called matriculations, which help them decide on a career and university. These universities are open to all Israeli citizens.

There are cultural and religious ceremonies that honor and include children, one of which is called bar mitzvah (for a boy) or bat mitzvah (for a girl). The translation means "son (or daughter) of the commandments." When boys reach the age of thirteen and girls reach the age of twelve, they are considered adult members of the community and are responsible for observing the biblical laws. Many families celebrate this coming-of-age with festive meals, sometimes in a synagogue, sometimes in a big hall with music and dancing.

Chasidic boys (boys who are dedicated to a religious life) study the Torah.

A Nation in the Army

Israel is a small country surrounded by Arab nations that have attacked from many directions over its short life. Therefore, the State of Israel has a strong army to defend its borders. After high school, most young men, and many young women, serve in the military. It is normal in daily life to see armed soldiers walking on the street or taking buses, shopping in malls, and dining in restaurants.

Citizens serve for one to three years. After that, the men will serve in the reserves for one month a year until the age of forty. Many of them receive training in special skills. Women who do not want to serve in the military have the option to do a year of national service, such as in a school or hospital.

Job Opportunities

Israel is known for its agriculture. Farmers grow and export fruits and flowers. In the Hebrew Bible, God promised a land that would be "a good land: a land of streams of water, of springs and underground water flowing in the valley and in the mountain, a land of wheat and barley, grapevines and figs, and pomegranates, a land of oil olives and [date] honey" (Deuteronomy 8:7–8, author's translation). These seven types of fruits are still treasured in Israel, as are many other kinds of crops, including almonds and walnuts, sunflowers (grown for their beauty and their seeds), citrus fruits, apples, avocados, and cherries.

In the days of the early pioneers, agricultural settlements called kibbutzim (the plural of *kibbutz,* meaning "communal settlement") were formed. Small communities of people lived and worked together to settle the land. They strove to make a society in which each person would work according to his or her ability and receive according to his or her need. The kibbutzim were an integral part of the beginnings of the State of Israel and a major source of produce, dairy, meat, and poultry. Kibbutzniks shared a common dining room, and children lived together in the children's houses. Although there are still kibbutzim, they are changing the way they work. Families have returned to living together. The cooperatives are no longer only agriculturally based. Some kibbutzim serve travelers with cabins or hotels. Many are industrialized and hire outside employees.

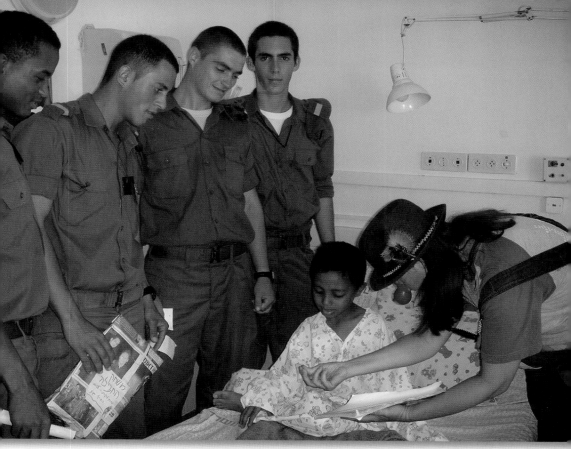

Medical clowning is a profession in Israel. Dream Doctor clowns go through courses to learn how to assist in hospitals. Respected as a valuable part of medical teams, they can help in procedures by easing the patients' pain or distress.

The high-tech and communication industries are lead by Israeli ingenuity. In 2011, Israel was working to produce 3D TV without the glasses. Hands-free cell phone technology and instant messaging are only some of Israel's contributions that have transformed the way the world connects.

Israel is a world leader in nanotechnology—working with powerful materials that are very, very small. Nanotechnology can be used in medicine (some are like mini-medical submarines that deliver drugs to cancer cells), the environment and energy (nano-sized solar cells are used to make inexpensive electricity), and security (in bomb sniffers and in monitoring water pollution), to name a few areas. Health and medical advances are also part of what Israel contributes to the world.

Benjamin Netanyahu (left) was born in Israel in 1949. He has served in the Israel Defense Force, as minister of finance, and as prime minister (1996–1999 and again beginning in 2009). Israeli President Shimon Peres (right) was born in Poland in 1923. He has served in several important government positions in Israel, including prime minister (1984–1986 and 1995–1996). He shared the Nobel Peace Prize in 1994 with Israel's Yitzhak Rabin and Palestinian leader Yasser Arafat.

Chapter 6

Famous Israelis

While the list of famous Israelis includes prizewinning scientists, mathematicians, and poets, many people like to know where their favorite actors and musicians are from. Here is a list of a few famous Israeli performers and politicians:

Aki Avni, an actor in *Homeland Security, Universal Soldier: Regeneration,* and *The Divided,* was born in Rehovot in 1967.

Actress **Gal Gadot** (*Fast Five, Fast & Furious, The Beautiful Life: TBL, Date Night*) was born in 1985 in Rosh Ha'ayin. She was crowned Miss Israel in 2004.

Topol, born in 1935 in Tel Aviv, played Tevye in the classic 1971 movie *Fiddler on the Roof* and in more than 2,500 performances of the stage show.

Actress **Ayelet Zurer** (*Angels and Demons, Vantage Point, Munich*), was also born in Tel Aviv.

Actress **Natalie Portman** (*Anywhere But Here; V for Vendetta; Star Wars: Episodes I, II, III; No Strings Attached; Black Swan;* and *Thor*), was born as Natalie Hershlag to an Israeli father and an American mother in Jerusalem. She moved to the United States when she was very young. Living in

Natalie Portman

New York, she was discovered at age 11 while eating pizza! She is well known for her role as Queen Amidala and Padmé in the Star Wars prequel films. She has worked in many films since then, and in 2011 she won an Academy Award for her performance in *Black Swan.*

The music of **Itzhak Perlman**, a classical violinist, can be heard in concerts and on the sound tracks of many well-known movies, including *Fantasia 2000, Small Wonders,* and *Schindler's List.* Perlman was born on August 31, 1945, in Tel Aviv. At three years old he asked his parents for a violin. At age four, he was stricken with polio, a disease that crippled his legs. Since that time, he has had to wear braces to walk, but it did not stop his brilliant career. After going to school at the Tel Aviv Academy of Music and New York's Juilliard, he began touring the world with his violin. He has performed for U.S. presidents (including Bill Clinton and Barack Obama) and other world dignitaries and is considered a superstar in his field. Perlman also volunteers for various charities, including those that help young people with music and those that fight polio.

Golda Meir was born in Kiev in 1898 and moved to the United States in 1906. In 1921 she and her husband moved to what was then called British Mandate Palestine. Three years later, she began her career in politics. She was actively involved in the formation of the State of Israel and became a member of the provisional government in 1948. She worked in various positions until, in 1969, Golda Meir became prime minister. She was the third woman in the world to hold such a high office.

Jesus of Nazareth, whom Christians call Jesus Christ (which means "Chosen"), may be the most famous Jew born in Israel. He was born around 2,000 years ago in Bethlehem. His mission was to spread the word of God. His teachings are found in the New Testament. In Christianity, Jesus is considered the messiah that God promised through the prophets of the Hebrew Bible (the Jewish religion believes that no man has yet fulfilled the role of messiah). Many Christian tourists take inspiring visits to Israel to see the places where Jesus walked, lived, preached, and died.

The Bible features many prophets (such as Jeremiah), kings (such as King David, who fought the giant Goliath), and warriors (such as the mighty Samson) who lived in Israel of old.

FYI FACT:

The Ethiopian Jews who were cut off from the rest of world Jewry for so long have an extra holiday they celebrate called Sigd. The holiday celebrates the acceptance of the Torah. Now that they are living in Israel, thousands of Ethiopian Jews gather each year in Jerusalem to observe this holiday, which has taken on new meaning since their return.

Celebrate!

No matter how busy life gets developing new technologies, creating music and movies, and improving politics, Israelis take time to celebrate a calendar full of holidays. Jewish holidays fall on dates according to the ancient Hebrew calendar, which is still in use. The Gregorian calendar, the one used in the United States, is based on the sun. The Hebrew calendar is based on the sun and the moon. The new moon signals the beginning of a month, so the full moon falls right in the middle of the month. Instead of adding a day for a leap year, the Hebrew calendar adds one whole month seven times in every nineteen years. Those years have thirteen months instead of twelve. The dates of Jewish holidays can vary on the secular calendar, but by adding a month, Chanukah always falls in the winter and Passover in the spring. Most of the population uses the Gregorian calendar for their day-to-day life, but religious Jews follow the Hebrew calendar. They may even use the Hebrew date when writing checks. For example, instead of writing April 15, 2012, the date would be 23 Nisan, 5772.

In Israel, the major Jewish holidays are also national holidays. Not surprisingly, most Jewish holidays are biblically based. Whether Israeli Jews are religious or not, they usually celebrate. Most holidays have some special foods associated with the time of year and meaning of the day. Children have a day or even a week or more off school. Here are some of the well-known and widely celebrated holidays, including non-biblical national holidays added by the State of Israel (Holocaust Day, Memorial Day, and Independence Day).

Jewish New Year, a two-day holiday called Rosh Hashanah, is the birthday of the creation of humankind. It is traditional to eat a festive meal, starting with apples dipped in honey as a blessing for a sweet new year. Other traditional foods are a round loaf of bread called challah, fish, and honey cake.

Yom Kippur, or the Day of Atonement, is a day of fasting and prayer. The holiest day of the year, it occurs eight days after Rosh Hashanah. It is said that God judges each person on Rosh Hashanah and then seals His judgment on Yom Kippur. It is a solemn day, but not a sad day.

Sukkot is a weeklong holiday spent in little huts that people build next to their homes. It is traditionally the time of the fall harvest. The hut, called a *succah*, is a reminder of the forty years of wandering the Jews did when they left the slavery of Egypt. The rabbis teach that sitting in a succah is like getting a hug from God. This is a time of family get-togethers and fun trips around the country.

The Torah is read in portions in synagogue services every week. *Simchat Torah* celebrates the completion of the yearlong reading of the Torah. When the last words are read, the reading cycle is begun again from the start. Dancing with the Torah scrolls is a big part of the celebration, expressing love for the teachings. It is very common to see smiling children bouncing on the shoulders of their fathers as they dance in circles with a Torah scroll.

For the Jewish New Year and Yom Kippur, a ram's horn called the shofar is blown in a series of 100 blasts. The horn seems to cry, "Wake up and live a life of goodness!"

Chanukah, one of the best-known holidays, is also called the Festival of Lights. About 400 years after the Syrian Greeks destroyed and defiled the First Temple in 586 BCE, a family known as the Maccabees fought to get back the Temple—and won. To rededicate the Temple, Judah Maccabee wanted to light the Temple Menorah (a special seven-branch candelabra). Although there was only enough pure oil to burn for one day, the menorah miraculously burned for eight days, when more pure oil could be prepared.

Chanukah always falls on the darkest time of the year (in the northern hemisphere)—when the days are the shortest and the night is the longest. When times are darkest, it is

Knesset Menorah bronze monument

important to remember that things will change, and there is always hope and a chance to light up the world.

Most Jews around the world continue to observe the tradition of lighting candles on Chanukah. The candles are usually placed in a window so that the light from them is shared with the world. In Israel, many Chanukah menorahs are lit and shine out into the darkness.

Since the miracle of light took place with olive oil, the traditional foods eaten at this time of year are fried, oily foods. Potato pancakes (latkes) and jelly doughnuts (*sufganiyot*) are especially enjoyed.

Tu B'shvat is the birthday of the trees. Many people plant trees on this day, honoring the gifts that trees bring the world. Many people eat a festive meal that includes the seven species that are listed in the

Bible as being indigenous to Israel (wheat, barley, grapes, figs, pomegranates, olives, and dates).

Purim celebrates the Scroll of Esther from the Talmud. The story takes place in Persia, where an evil man named Haman convinces the king to decree death to all Jews. Around the same time, the king searches the kingdom for a new queen, and he chooses a Jewish girl named Esther. She does not reveal her background at the beginning. Through a series of miracles—and the bravery of Esther and her uncle Mordechai—the decree is reversed and the Jews are saved.

Children dressed for Purim

At Purim, the Scroll of Esther is read in homes and synagogues, and whenever the name of Haman is read, everyone makes loud noises. The idea is to blot out evil. Children dress up in costumes (because things are not always as they seem!), and neighborhoods buzz as baskets of food are delivered to neighbors and friends. Gifts to the poor are another part of the observance of Purim. A traditional cookie called hamantashen is eaten to celebrate this holiday. These three-cornered cookies have a fruit filling—poppyseed, plum, apricot, or any other kind of jam can fill this favorite, and they are often topped with powdered sugar, too. The name of the cookie means "Haman's hat," taken from the evil Haman.

Passover is the remembrance of the Exodus from Egypt, when God took the Jewish people out of slavery. Families gather for the Passover

Seder, a special meal during which the Passover Haggadah—a small book that tells the story of the Exodus—is recited. Traditional symbolic foods are served and displayed, including bitter herbs and matzoh, a type of flat bread. In their hasty departure from slavery in Egypt, the Jews did not have time to let the bread rise (leaven); to remember this hardship, leavened foods are forbidden for the entire week of Passover—including bread and cake, breakfast cereals, and even soups that contain flour. The month before Passover is a national cleaning frenzy, as people scour their homes to make sure no leavened products, not even a crumb, can be found. Prepackaged foods must have certification that they were carefully made according to the biblical law, and they will say "Kosher for Passover."

Lag B'Omer is known for being a day of bonfires and celebration. Starting on the second day of Passover, the days are counted leading to *Shavuot*. The first thirty-two days of the counting is a somber time. People generally do not marry during that time. On the thirty-third day of the counting, that changes. Lag B'Omer is the start of the wedding season.

Shavuot celebrates the Jewish people receiving the Torah on Mount Sinai. People stay up all night studying the Torah to show their appreciation for this divine gift. Dairy foods—especially cheesecake—are traditional on this day. Shavuot also coincides with the spring harvest.

Holocaust Remembrance Day commemorates those who were murdered by the Nazis during World War II. A memorial siren is heard in all the cities. People stop what they are doing, even if they are driving, and stand for two minutes of silent remembrance.

Memorial Day is dedicated to the soldiers of the Israel Defense Forces who have fallen while defending the country. The memorial siren is sounded on this day also, and many people visit cemeteries to pay their respects to the fallen heroes.

Independence Day, called *Yom Ha'atzma'ut* in Hebrew, is a celebration of the birthday of the State of Israel on May 14, 1948. The day is usually filled with barbecues and fireworks, just as it is on Independence Day in the United States.

Weddings in Israel

Of course weddings are a time for celebration and joy. Before a wedding, just as in the United States, there are parties for the couple and wedding showers for the bride. There are other traditions and rituals depending on the family's religious observance, such as whether they are Sephardic or Ashkenazi, and on where the families are from. For example, brides whose families come from Yemen wear the traditional Yemenite headdress. Sephardic Jews have a henna party. In this ritual, a natural dye from the henna plant is mixed and spread on the palms of the bride and groom and sometimes on the palms of some of the guests.

Ashkenazi grooms have an *aufruf* on the Sabbath before the wedding. In this ceremony, the groom is called to bless and stand next to the Torah while it is being read in the synagogue. The congregants throw candy at the groom to symbolize a sweet life as a married man. (This is a very popular ritual with the children, who gather around in anticipation of scrambling to gather the loot!)

It is not unusual to see brides in their gowns at the Western Wall in Jerusalem, where they may go to pray right before their wedding.

The traditional Jewish wedding is performed under a canopy called a chuppah. The chuppah is open on all four sides to

symbolize the couple's commitment to build a welcoming home. The tent of their ancestor Abraham had entrances on all four sides so that guests would be welcomed no matter from what direction they came.

A rabbi leads the wedding ceremony, helping the couple perform the rituals and fulfill the laws. Just as the bride has a ring that encircles her finger, she walks around the groom seven times to symbolize Godly light. The groom presents her with a ring and a *ketubah,* a wedding contract, in which he promises to provide for her. The ceremony closes with seven blessings for the bride and groom. The blessings are made over a glass of wine, and the couple drinks from the glass. Then the glass is wrapped in cloth and placed on the ground. The groom stomps on it to break it.

This tradition reminds those present that even in moments of the greatest joy, there is sadness because the Temple in Jerusalem is destroyed. When the glass breaks, the crowd shouts, *"Mazel tov!"* "Congratulations!"

For Jews, there is no holier spot than the Western Wall, called the *Kotel* in Hebrew. A fourth-century rabbi taught that God's presence would never leave the only remaining outer wall of the original Temple. The cracks between the large stones are stuffed with thousands of tiny notes, written prayers, as a way to call out to God.

Chapter

8

Jerusalem of Gold

At the heart of Israel is Jerusalem—the ancient capital of the Jewish people and the modern capital of the State of Israel. It is where King Solomon built the Temple, and it is the city that powerful empires, long since perished, fought bloody battles to conquer. Built, destroyed, and rebuilt over thousands of years, it has many layers of roads and buildings from the Jews, Romans, Byzantines, Muslims, Crusaders, and Turks. Holy to three of the world's religions, Jerusalem is on nearly every traveler's list of places to see. The winding, narrow, cobblestone roads of the Old City of Jerusalem have witnessed thousands of years of war, bloodshed, prayer, and celebration. Modern Jerusalem is home to museums, medicine, and the hustle and bustle of big-city life.

"Jerusalem of Gold" is a popular song that stirs the hearts of many. *"Jerusalem of gold, of copper and light; Behold, for all your songs, I am your violin."* But is Jerusalem really gold? Built using what is called Jerusalem Stone, the city, old and new, has a unified look. The stones are closer to white, but as the sun sets, the golden glow reflects off the pale stones, and Jerusalem really does look golden.

Celebrations abound. Young men in white knitted skullcaps sometimes blast music from vans and dance in the streets. People meet for dance classes in the open-air market (the *shuk*) at night when the stores are closed. Even the zoo takes a spiritual turn in this special city: it is called the Biblical Zoo, and features a replica of Noah's Ark.

The Israel Festival in Jerusalem attracts hundreds of performers from around the world, as well as Israel's own performers. There are shows on stages and in the streets, from children's shows to jazz concerts.

The walled, ancient city of King David, called the Old City, opens the imagination to a time that was and to a future filled with hope and promise. The Old City is divided into four quarters: the Jewish Quarter, Armenian Quarter, Christian Quarter, and Muslim Quarter.

Jewish Quarter

When the Jews were expelled from the Land of Israel two thousand years ago, they never stopped singing about Jerusalem. At the end of the Passover Seder, Jews all around the world say, "Next year in Jerusalem." Jerusalem is the symbol of all that could be right in the world, the potential of mankind to rise to its best. It was the home of the Temple, where God's presence rested.

Where the Temple stood two thousand years ago, one outer wall still remains standing in the heart of the old city. It is called the Western Wall. As early as the eleventh century, Jews came to grieve the destruction of the Temple. Jewish tears and mourning prompted outsiders to name the place the Wailing Wall. Some wept for joy to be so close to it, especially in 1967 when Jerusalem was again opened freely to Jewish worshipers. This wall is the site of countless visitors, and prayers pour from their hearts.

The area at the wall is divided so that men and women can pray separately, which is the Orthodox way. Some people sway and move as they pray. Just as a flame flickers, so the fire of prayer can change and move a person. As people leave the wall, they walk backward for several paces as a sign of respect—they do not turn their back on God's presence.

On the Sabbath and holidays, Jerusalemites and visitors wear their finest clothes and come to dance and pray. It is not unusual to see bearded Chasidim in their white shirts and black coats dancing with soldiers in their khaki greens, guns slung over their shoulders.

The weekend in Israel is really only one day, and that is Saturday. Saturday is called *Shabbat* (shah-BAHT) which is the Hebrew word for Sabbath. The Torah teaches that the world was created in six days and that God rested on the seventh day, so that's the day everyone takes off. For some people, the Sabbath is the day to run errands or go to the beach. For others, it's a spiritual journey into another mindset. Jerusalem, like some other cities and towns, pretty much shuts down. Hardly a store is open and hardly a car drives on the street as a special kind of peace blankets the city. It is a happy time for friends and family to eat festive meals together, invite guests, talk, and learn.

The Armenian Quarter

The roots of the Armenian Quarter probably began in the fourth century, when a small group of Armenians came to be near the early Christian sites. At its peak in 1948, over 16,000 Armenians lived in this part of the city, but that number has dwindled to about 1,000. St. James Armenian Convent, with its complex of churches, a library, a school, a museum of Armenian art and culture, and gardens, is one of the main attractions in this quarter. Colorful Armenian pottery is popular with tourists.

Christian Quarter

For the Christians, Jerusalem is the place where Jesus preached, was crucified, and, according to the Christian Bible (or New Testament), was resurrected. Christian prophecy says that Jesus will one day return to Jerusalem.

Jerusalem is home to a variety of churches, where services are held in at least thirteen languages for more than twelve types of Christian worship. The Garden of Gethsemane at the foot of the Mount of Olives is known as the place where Jesus prayed with his disciples before his crucifixion. The Church of the Holy Sepulcher, the holiest site for Christians, is in the Old City of Jerusalem. Every year, thousands of Christian pilgrims flock to Jerusalem to walk the final steps of Jesus, ending at this church. Worshipers kneel to touch the spot where he was laid to rest, many kissing the spot and weeping. Church bells have been ringing since the fourth century at this site of Christian pilgrimage, where the tomb (sepulcher) of Jesus is said to lie.

In the Church of the Sepulcher, people wait in line to enter under the Altar of the Crucifixion to touch the site where Jesus died on the cross. The church is located on the traditional site of Golgotha, the crucifixion and burial site of Jesus.

Muslim Quarter

While Mecca and Medina are the holiest cities to the Muslims, Jerusalem has a place in their hearts as well. The Koran, the holy book of the Muslim faith, tells about the night journey of Muhammad the prophet. Tradition holds that he was taken by an angel from the great place of prayer in Mecca to the remote place of prayer in Jerusalem. From there he rose to heaven.

The skyline reveals Muslim mosques, with their domed roofs and tall minarets calling worshipers to prayer. With its striking gold dome, and mosaics inside and out, the Dome of the Rock (right) has become a landmark in Jerusalem.

From ancient times to modern, Jerusalem has been the great heart of the tiny country of Israel. While the city hustles and bustles with buildings and technology, the ancient mysteries still tug at the souls of visitors and citizens alike. Under Jewish rule, Jerusalem—and the rest of this democratic country—has become a safe place for all worshipers.

Israeli Hamantashen

This jelly-filled cookie delights Israelis every spring when it's time for the holiday of Purim. The following family recipe is over 100 years old. Be creative. You can add almond extract to the dough or use any kind of pie filling or preserves that you like.

3 eggs
½ cup sugar
pinch salt
½ cup oil
¼ cup water (or orange juice)
2 cups flour
2 rounded teaspoons baking powder
Jam or other filling

1. In a bowl, mix together the eggs, sugar, salt, oil, and water (or orange juice).
2. Stir the baking powder into the flour, then add them to the bowl of liquids. Mix with a spoon.
3. Sprinkle some flour on a cutting board, then dump the dough in the middle and knead lightly. When you feel it's enough (not too firm), separate the dough into four pieces.
4. Roll out each piece, adding more flour if it sticks. Use a 3-inch cookie cutter or the rim of a glass to get round pieces.
5. Add a rounded teaspoon of filling to the center of each circle, then pinch the edges together in three places to form a triangle. It should be a little open in the middle to show the filling.
6. Bake at 350°F for about 15 minutes, until light golden brown.

Israeli

Hamsa

The hamsa, which is a decoration used in both Jewish and Muslim life, is a decorative hand that is supposed to remind us of the hand of God, the hand that protects and blesses. The hamsa is a traditional piece of art that can come in the form of jewelry, drawings, or wood, ceramic, or metal hanging pieces. The hand can be facing up (up is more common in Israel) or down, and is a symbol used all across the Middle East and Africa.

Choose any design or color that looks nice to you, but you might consider using popular symbols such as an eye or a fish. The eye is to protect from the "evil eye." There is not some evil eyeball floating around—this is just to remind you not to give people dirty looks that could hurt others, and to remind you that the mean stares of someone else do not have to hurt you! The shape of a fish is also found often, because fish do not gossip, nor do they ever give the evil eye.

Materials
A piece of flat Styrofoam
Scissors, glue, and a variety of decorations, such as colored felt; paint and puff paint; sequins; stickers; dried flowers, buttons, or feathers; construction paper cut into different shapes
Fishing line or other string
Wooden skewer

Instructions
1. Draw the shape of a hamsa (you can trace your hand) onto the foam and carefully cut it out.
2. Paint the template or cut out felt shapes from the same template and glue them over the Styrofoam hamsa.
3. Now decorate your hamsa. Be creative!
4. When you have it just how you like it, use the skewer to make a hole through the foam. Thread the string through the hole so that you can hang it up. You can also thread beads onto the string and tie knots to keep them in place.

You could also make this project in clay using a slab: simply cut the slab in the shape of a hamsa, pierce a hole for hanging later, then either draw or press shapes or designs into the clay's surface. Under **adult** supervision, fire, glaze, and fire. You can create beaded hangers as suggested above.

BCE	(Some of these dates are approximate)
1850	Abraham journeys to Canaan (the Holy Land) when God promises that he will found a great nation.
1700	Jews move to Egypt to escape famine and eventually become enslaved.
1250	In the Exodus, Jews leave Egypt under the leadership of Moses.
1050	The Kingdom of Israel is founded.
1004–965	King David reigns. He conquers Jerusalem and makes the city the capital of Israel.
960	David's son King Solomon builds the First Temple in Jerusalem.
721	Assyrian King Sargon II captures Israel.
586	Babylonians under Nebuchadnezzar capture Judah and Jerusalem, destroy the temple, and force Jews to go to Babylon.
538	Persian King Cyrus captures Babylon and allows Jews to return to Jerusalem.
536	Construction begins on Second Temple.
166	Revolt led by Judas Maccabee leads to Jewish independence.
63	Romans take control of what is now called Judea.
CE	
66–70	Jews revolt against Roman rule; Second Temple is destroyed, leaving only the Western Wall.
132–135	Jews revolt; Diaspora begins; Judea is renamed Syria Palestina.
610–632	Muhammad founds the religion of Islam.
638	Caliph Umar declares that Muhammad ascended to heaven from Jerusalem at the site of the Temple Mount, making the city the third-most holy site in Islam.
1099	Christians in First Crusade capture Jerusalem and slaughter most of its Jewish and Muslim populations.
1187	Muslim leader Saladin recaptures Jerusalem and expels the Crusaders.
1492	During the Inquisition, Spain expels nearly all of its Jewish population.
1881	The assassination of Czar Alexander II in Russia leads to pogroms against Jews and sparks a massive Jewish exodus out of Russia.
1882	The First Aliyah begins.
1903	The Second Aliyah begins.
1909	Tel Aviv is founded.
1917	British Foreign Secretary Arthur Balfour expresses support for a Jewish homeland in the Balfour Declaration.
1919	The Third Aliyah begins soon after the end of World War I.
1920	The League of Nations grants Great Britain a mandate over Palestine; the Ottoman Empire ends.
1921	The British create a separate mandate for Transjordan, which creates the country of Jordan. The French create Syria and Lebanon.
1924	The Fourth Aliyah begins.
1929	The Fifth Aliyah begins.
1933	Adolf Hitler becomes German dictator; first concentration camp is established at Dachau, Germany. More Jews join the Fifth Aliyah.

1939	British issue White Paper that severely curtails further Jewish immigration; World War II begins when Germany invades Poland.
1945	World War II in Europe ends; six million Jews have been murdered; homeless Jews and others begin entering displaced persons camps.
1947	The United Nations General Assembly votes to partition Palestine into two states.
1948	Israel declares its independence. David Ben-Gurion becomes its first prime minister. Israel defeats invading armies from five Arab countries.
1949	Chaim Weizmann is elected Israel's first President of the State of Israel; Israel signs armistice agreements with the countries that attacked it.
1964	Arab League founds the Palestine Liberation Organization (PLO), with the stated goal of destroying Israel.
1967	Israel defeats several Arab nations in the Six-Day War and more than doubles its size, primarily by capturing the Sinai Peninsula. Jerusalem is unified.
1969	Golda Meir becomes Israeli prime minister. Yasser Arafat is elected chairman of PLO's executive committee.
1973	Following initial reverses after being attacked by Syria and Egypt, Israel wins the Yom Kippur War; Ben-Gurion dies.
1978	The Camp David Accords lead to diplomatic recognition of Israel by Egypt and the return of the Sinai Peninsula to Egypt.
1982	Israel invades Lebanon; Lebanese president-elect Bashir Gemayel is assassinated; Christians massacre hundreds of Palestinians in two refugee camps in retaliation.
1987	The First Intifada (uprising) breaks out in Gaza; it lasts until 1990.
1993	Israel and the PLO agree to mutual recognition and transition to Palestinian self-rule in the West Bank and Gaza Strip in the Oslo Accords, but the agreement is not carried out.
1995	Israeli Prime Minister Yitzhak Rabin, one architect of the Oslo Accords, is assassinated by an Israeli extremist. His successor, Shimon Peres, is defeated by Benjamin Netanyahu, who opposes the agreement.
1996	The PLO formally revokes all clauses in its founding charter calling for the dissolution of Israel.
2000	The Second Intifada begins.
2004	Yasser Arafat dies.
2006	Iranian President Mahmoud Ahmadinejad labels the Holocaust a "myth" and calls for the elimination of Israel; Israel attacks Lebanon after Palestinian guerrillas based there kidnap two Israeli soldiers.
2007	Palestinian factions Hamas and Fatah fight each other; Fatah controls the West Bank and Hamas controls the Gaza Strip.
2008	Israel celebrates its 60th anniversary.
2009	Tel Aviv celebrates its 90th anniversary.
2011	Israeli security forces clash with Palestinian protesters storming border areas. Fatah and Hamas factions sign a unity agreement.

Books

Burgan, Michael. *Teens in Israel* (Global Connections Series). Minnesota: Compass Point Books, 2007.

Hintz, Martin. *Israel: Enchantment of the World*. New York: Children's Press, 2006.

Smith, Debbie. *Israel: The Culture* (Lands, Peoples, and Cultures). New York: Crabtree Publishing, 2008.

Sofer, Barbara. *Keeping Israel Safe: Serving in the Israel Defense Forces*. Minnesota: Kar-Ben Publishing, 2008.

Whiting, Jim. *The Creation of Israel*. Hockessin, Delaware: Mitchell Lane Publishers, 2007.

Young, Emma. *National Geographic Countries of the World: Israel*. New York: National Geographic Children's Books, 2008.

Works Consulted

This book is based on the author's personal experience living in Israel, and on the following sources:

The Armenian Patriarchate of St. James, Jerusalem, http://www.armenian-patriarchate.org/page6.html

CIA. *The World Factbook:* "Israel." https://www.cia.gov/library/publications/the-world-factbook/geos/is.html

Garton, Christine. "Itzhak Perlman Says We Are 'This Close' to Ending Polio for Good." *USA Today,* February 1, 2011. http://yourlife.usatoday.com/mind-soul/doing-good/kindness/post/2011/02/itzhak-perlman-says-we-are-this-close-to-ending-polio-for-good/141014/1

Go Jerusalem. "The Ethiopian Holiday of Sigd." http://www.gojerusalem.com/article_602/The-Ethiopian-Holiday-of-Sigd-

Holyland Network. "Jerusalem Churches." http://www.holylandnetwork.com/jerusalem/churches.htm

Hula Valley International Bird Festival http://www.hulabirdfestival.org

"IDF Field Hospital in Haiti." *CBS News,* video clip, January 19, 2010. http://www.youtube.com/watch?v=FCx0SKPG9V0

In Israel. "Table of Average Temperatures in Major Cities in Israel." http://www.inisrael.com/tour/weather/index.html

Israel Ministry of Foreign Affairs. "Facets of Israeli Economy—Biotechnology." November 1, 2002. http://www.mfa.gov.il/mfa/mfaarchive/2000_2009/2002/11/facets%20of%20the%20israeli%20economy-%20biotechnology

———. "Facts About Israel: History." November 28, 2010. http://www.mfa.gov.il/MFA/Facts+About+Israel/History/Facts+about+Israel-+History.htm

———. "A Free People in Our Land: Israel—Democracy in the Middle East." April 1, 2005. http://www.mfa.gov.il/MFA/Government/Facts+about+Israel-+The+State/A+Free+People+in+Our+Land-+Israel+-+Democracy+in+the+Middle+East.htm

Israel Ministry of Tourism. "Tel Aviv." http://www.tourism.gov.il/Tourism_Euk/Destinations/Tel+Aviv/General+Info+-+Tel+Aviv.htm

Israel Science and Technology. http://www.science.co.il/

Israel Up Close. "Israel Contributions." http://www.israelupclose.org/categories/israel_contributions.html

Itzhak Perlman http://www.itzhakperlman.com

Jewish National Fund. "Forestry and Ecology." http://www.jnf.org/work-we-do/our-projects/forestry-ecology/

Jewish Virtual Library. "Golda Meir." http://www.jewishvirtuallibrary.org/jsource/biography/meir.html

———. "The History of the Ethiopian Jews." http://www.jewishvirtuallibrary.org/jsource/Judaism/ejhist.html

———. "The Kibbutz." http://www.jewishvirtuallibrary.org/jsource/Society_&_Culture/kibbutz.html

———. "Western Wall" or "Wailing Wall"? http://www.jewishvirtuallibrary.org/jsource/History/wallname.html

Kloosterman, Karin. "Israel's Nanotech Industry Takes Off." *Israel National News.com,* March 20, 2009. http://www.israelnationalnews.com/News/News.aspx/130532

"Medical Clowning." *CNN,* International Edition, video, January 7, 2010. http://edition.cnn.com/video/data/2.0/video/international/2009/12/28/vital.signs.medical.clowning.cnn.html

Metz, Helen Chapin, ed. *Israel: A Country Study.* Washington: GPO for the Library of Congress, 1988. http://countrystudies.us/israel/

Mount Hermon http://www.hermon.com/mt_hermon/

Neot Kedumim. http://www.neot-kedumim.org.il/

The Nobel Peace Prize 1994: Yasser Arafat, Shimon Peres, Yitzhak Rabin http://nobelprize.org/nobel_prizes/peace/laureates/1994/peres-bio.html

Palestine Facts. http://www.palestinefacts.org/pf_early_palestine_name_origin.php

"Revisiting the Violinist, Itzhak Perlman, Virtuoso, Now Conductor, Too." *60 Minutes,* January 17, 2000. http://www.cbsnews.com/stories/2000/01/17/60II/main150331.shtml

Shamah, David. "Israeli Nanotech Provides Green Electricity." Video. December 24, 2007. http://www.israel21c.org/200712241818/environment/israeli-nanotech-provides-green-electricity-video

Technion: Israel Institute of Technology, "Fast Facts" http://pard.technion.ac.il/fastfacts/FramsFactsE.asp?myret=main

Virtual Israel Experience. "Makhtesh Ramon." http://www.jewishvirtuallibrary.org/jsource/vie/Ramon.html

On the Internet

Aish.com, Assyrian Conquest http://www.aish.com/jl/h/48937787.html

Aish.com, Star of David http://www.aish.com/jl/sp/k/48942436.html

Aish.com, Timeline, Four Thousand Years of Jewish History at a Glance http://www.aish.com/jl/h/48964541.html

Eye On Israel: Wildlife in Israel http://www.eyeonisrael.com/israel-wildlife.html

HebCal Jewish Calendar Date Converter http://www.hebcal.com/converter/

Israel Government Portal http://www.gov.il/firstgov/English

Israel Museums http://ilmuseums.com/

Israel Tourism Government Portal http://www.tourism.gov.il/Tourism_Eng

Israel Tourism Guide: Hermon http://tourism.index.co.il/siteFiles/1/60/260968.asp

Jewish Virtual Library http://www.jewishvirtuallibrary.org/

My Jewish Learning: Hamsa http://www.myjewishlearning.com/beliefs/Issues/Magic_and_the_Supernatural/Practices_and_Beliefs/Amulets/Hamsa.shtml

Travel for Kids, Fun to Do in Israel http://travelforkids.com/Funtodo/Israel/

PHOTO CREDITS: Cover, pp. 8, 20, 22, 24, 29, 31, 32, 40, 41, 46, 49, 54, 55, 57—cc-by-sa; pp. 1, 2, 6–7, 23, 25, 28, 30 (bottom), 45, 50—Photos.com/Getty Images; pp. 2–3, 30 (top)—Jonathan Hanig; p. 10—Rembrandt Harmensz. van Rijn; p. 14—Dmitri Kessel/Time Life Pictures/Getty Images; p. 16—U.S. Central Intelligence Agency; p. 17—AFP/Getty Images; p. 33—Laya Saul; p. 35—Tom Stoddart Archive/Getty Images; p. 38—Emil Salman/AFP/Getty Images; p. 42—Gali Tibbon/AFP/Getty Images; p. 48—Buccina Studios/Getty Images. Every effort has been made to locate all copyright holders of material used in this book. If any errors or omissions have occurred, corrections will be made in future editions of the book.

aliyah (ah-lee-YAH)—Hebrew word that means "ascending" or "going up," the return of the Jews to Israel.

anti-Semitism (AN-tee-SEH-mih-tis-em)—Hatred of Jewish people.

apostle (uh-PAH-sul)—A follower of Jesus.

autonomous (aw-TAH-nuh-mus)—Independent or self-governing.

Chasid (hah-SID)—A Jew who strictly observes biblical commandments and is dedicated to a religious life; the plural is *Chasidim*.

covenant (KUH-vuh-nunt)—A contract or binding agreement.

crucify (KROO-sih-fy)—An ancient form of torture and execution by nailing a person to a cross.

Diaspora (dee-AS-por-uh)—After the Babylonian exile, the Jews who were dispersed and lived outside their ancestral homeland.

exile (EK-zyl)—To cast someone out of his or her native country and forbid him or her to return.

henna (HEN-uh)—A natural plant extract that dyes the hair and skin a reddish color.

Holocaust (HALL-uh-kost)—The mass murder of the Jewish people by the Nazis.

idolatry (eye-DAH-luh-tree)—Worshiping idols (statues of gods).

immigrate (IM-uh-grayt)—To move into a new country.

omnipotent (om-NIH-puh-tunt)—All seeing, all knowing, all powerful (God).

pilgrimage (PIL-gruh-mij)—A journey to fulfill a religious or spiritual mission.

pogrom (pah-GROM)—A massacre of helpless people. The word has Yiddish origins and comes from the Russian word meaning "to devastate."

potential (poh-TEN-shul)—The possibility to develop something positive for the future.

prophet (PRAH-fet)—A person who, through special visions, brings messages from God.

quota (KWOH-tah)—A limited number of people or things allowed.

refugee (REH-fyoo-jee)—Someone looking for a place to live after being forced to leave his or her home because of war or other hardship.

resurrect (reh-zer-EKT)—To bring back to life.

sabra (SAH-brah)—A native-born Israeli; the fruit of the prickly pear cactus.

secular (SEH-kyoo-lur)—Not specifically spiritual or religious.

tallith (TAH-lis)—Prayer shawl.

Torah (TOR-uh)—The Hebrew Bible; one of the holy books of Judaism.

Zionist (ZY-uh-nist)—Having to do with creating a Jewish state or country.

INDEX

Laya Saul grew up in California. As a child she saved her coins to be able to buy trees that would be planted in Israel. After high school, she spent a year there. Something stirred inside her and she felt at home. Then, in 2003, Laya, her husband, and their children moved to Israel, where they adopted a dog and a cat. Her family has planted four fruit trees in their yard. She liked writing this book because there are so many wonderful things to know about Israel and the people who live there.

Laya, also known as Aunt Laya, wrote a book for teens called *You Don't Have to Learn Everything the Hard Way*. She has also written several other books for Mitchell Lane Publishers, including World Crafts and Recipes: *Recipe and Craft Guide to Israel*.